MARTIN'S
DREAM

For Yohannes and his dream of books
in the hands of Ethiopian children —J. K.

To Michael and Amanda
—A. J.-B.

ISBN: 978-0-545-23495-5

12 11 10 9 8 7 6 5 4 3 2 1   10 11 12 13 14 15/0

Printed in the U.S.A.   40

First Scholastic printing, January 2010

Designed by Lisa Vega
The text of this book was set in 24pt Century Oldstyle BT.

MARTIN'S DREAM

By Jane Kurtz

ILLUSTRATED BY
Amy June Bates

SCHOLASTIC INC.
New York Toronto London Auckland
Sydney Mexico City New Delhi Hong Kong

Martin Luther King
had a heart
so bold and strong.

He came one day
with things to say
to Washington, D.C.,
in 1963.

Two hundred thousand people
came together
on that day.

By bus, on skates,
from many states,
they came in like a stream,
looking for a dream.

They looked up at the face
of the man
who once declared,
in 1863,
all slaves must now be free.

But a law is just a start.
What can change a heart?

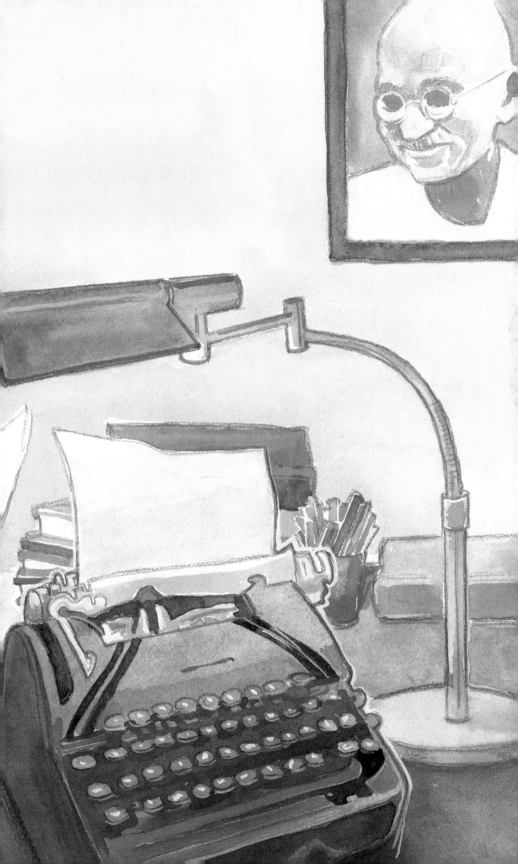

Martin Luther King
stood tall before them all.

He said
when it was time to vote
or play or work or ride,
no one should be outside.

The color of our skin
must not push us out or in.

Martin Luther King
almost sang
his words that day.

His voice rang out,
almost a shout.

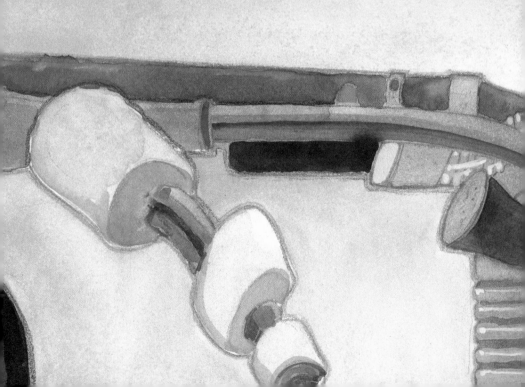

When things are fair
everywhere,
then people will be free.
We will have liberty.

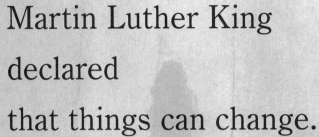

Martin Luther King
declared
that things can change.

Children can stand
hand in hand,
and we should all be able
to sit at the same table.

Martin Luther King
had a dream
so strong and clear,
some went away
changed that day.